He's at it again. Everybody's favorite kid is up to more of his merry pranks and hilarious antics. *DENNIS THE MENACE, HAPPY HALF-PINT* is stirring up a gallon of side-splitting, rib-tickling fun!

Also by Hank Ketcham:

Dennis the Menace—
  HERE COMES TROUBLE   13634 $1.50

Dennis the Menace—
  DRIVING MOTHER UP THE WALL   14134 $1.25

Dennis the Menace—
  HOUSEHOLD HURRICANE   13679 $1.25

Dennis the Menace—
  TEACHER'S THREAT   13643 $1.25

Dennis the Menace
HAPPY HALF-PINT

by Hank Ketcham

FAWCETT GOLD MEDAL • NEW YORK

DENNIS THE MENACE, HAPPY HALF-PINT

Published by Fawcett Gold Medal Books, a unit of CBS Publications, the Consumer Publishing Division of CBS Inc., by arrangement with Random House, Inc., in association with Hall Editions, Inc.

DENNIS THE MENACE, HAPPY HALF-PINT was originally published by Random House, Inc. This expanded edition, prepared especially for Fawcett Publications, Inc., contains 62 cartoons which did not appear in the original, higher-priced editions.

ISBN: 0-449-13649-3

Printed in the United States of America

27   26   25   24   23   22   21   20   19

"MMMM, BOY! IT SURE SMELLS *HAPPY* IN HERE!"

"... AN' MRS. PAULSON SAYS YOU WON'T EVER HAVE TO WORRY 'BOUT HIM HAVIN' BABIES. HE'S BEEN *SPRAYED!*"

"I'LL BET YOU'D HOWL, TOO, IF I MADE *YOU* SLEEP OUTSIDE!"

"OH, IS THAT *YOURS*? I WAS WONDERIN' WHERE HE GOT THAT OLD FASHIONED SHOE!"

"WHATTA YA READIN', MR. WILSON? HUH? WHATTA YA READIN'? HUH? HUH, MR. WILSON? HUH? MR. WILSON? . . . . "

"WE GOT ANY MORE FLASH BULBS? ME 'N STEW ARE HAVIN' A *RAY GUN* BATTLE!"

"ARE YOU TRYING TO TELL ME THE SUN IS BIGGER'N THE WHOLE *WORLD*? ARE YOU TRYIN' TO TELL ME *THAT*?"

"GO AHEAD AN' **TRY** IT. MARGARET! I *DARE* YA!"

"YOU GOT ANYTHING THAT WILL GROW HAIR ON A WHITE RAT'S TAIL?"

"...AND IT'S GOT A RED LIGHT AN' A GREEN LIGHT AN'....AW, HECK, I GUESS IT'S GONE NOW...."

"IT'S GOT NOTHING TO DO WITH THE WAY I ACT. *LOTS* OF PEOPLE HAVE CRAB GRASS!"

"HI, DAD! THOUGHT I'D WATCH A COUPLE MINUTES WHILE MOM IS FILLIN' THE BATHTUB!"

"I'LL SHAKE HANDS IF YOU WILL."

"....I SAID PUT YOUR MOTHER ON THE PHONE! WHAT?
YES, I'M STILL MAD AT YOU! HELLO? DENNIS? *DENNIS!*..."

"LOOK, I'M SORRY I LOST MY TEMPER, HENRY. AND I WANT YOU TO KNOW I'M GOING TO BUY DENNIS ANOTHER DRUM."

"WANNA BOX A COUPLE ROUNDS 'FORE BREAKFAST?"

"YOU SURE HATE TO SEE A ROOM LOOK *RELAXED!*"

"HI, MR. WILSON! I'LL ONLY BE A *MINUTE!*"

"MR. WILSON SAYS IF HE HAD A NICE HOUSE LIKE MINE, HE'D STAY INSIDE *ALL* THE TIME!"

"NOW DON'T YELL AT ME THIS TIME AN' MAYBE I'LL *MAKE* IT!"

"SURE LUCKY I WENT ALONG! DAD GOT THE *BIGGEST* SCORE HE EVER MADE!"

'I SURE WAS **SURPRISED**! SOME DOPE TOL' ME HE WAS A **SISSY**!'

"BECAUSE SHE'S AFRAID YOU MIGHT BREAK IT, DEAR."

"I'LL BE COWBOY BOB, YOU BE BAD BART, AN' MR. WILSON'LL BE THE FAT GUY WHO SAYS 'THEY WENT *THATAWAY*'!"

"HELLO, GRANDPA? LISTEN, WHY DON'T YA COME OVER AN'
SPOIL ME FOR A FEW DAYS?"

"LOOK WHAT GRANDPA BROUGHT ME! *BONGO DRUMS!*"

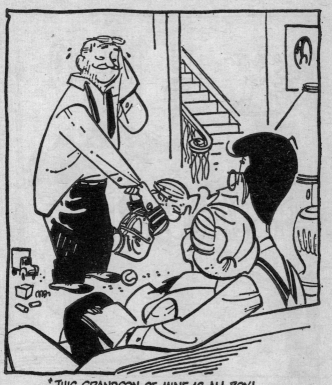

"THIS GRANDSON OF MINE IS ALL BOY! AND I'M ALL *IN!* GOODNIGHT, KIDS."

"IT'S SURE NICE TO HAVE SOMEBODY TO TALK TO, GRANDPA. MOM 'N DAD GET **SORE** IF I WAKE _THEM_ UP!"

"DON'T WORRY. YOU KNOW HOW BIG PEOPLE ARE ... THEY GET TIRED OF THINGS FAST."

"DID YOU EVER THINK OF ALL THE LEMONADE YOU COULDA MADE WITH THIS WATER?"

"THEY SLEEP NEXT DOOR. *LIVE* HERE."

"I'M BABY SITTING THE LITTLE BOY NEXT DOOR, ONLY HE'S *NOT*, AND I THOUGHT.....OH, *THERE* YOU ARE!"

'SURE, I'LL TELL YA WHY I NEED A NEW CAR. 'CAUSE I JUST GOT BEAT BY A *TRICYCLE!* *THAT'S* WHY!"

"CAN I STAY HERE WHILE MY MOM GETS OVER A BUSTED VASE?"

"MY KINDERGARTER TEACHER SAYS ANY BIG PEOPLE THAT WOULD HIT LITTLE KIDS IS *SICK!*"

"WHAT *HAPPENED*? I LIKED THE *BROWN* COAT. *YOU* LIKED THE BROWN COAT... HOW COME YA GOT THE *BLUE* COAT?"

"ON THE ROAD TO MANDA *WHO*?"

"HOW CAN I GET TO HEAVEN IF I DON'T GET MY WINGS 'TIL I *GET* THERE?"

"THE KIDS DECIDED THAT YOU WERE THE MOM WE HAVE THE MOST FUN PLAYIN' IN THE HOUSE OF!"

"WELL, HI, MOM! CARE FOR A GLASS OF MILK?"

"BUT WHAT MAKES YA THINK _I_ DID IT?"

"BOY, WAIT'LL *SALLY* SEES THIS!"

"THEN HOW 'BOUT A PENNY? I'LL PULL IT FOR A PENNY!
OKAY? JUST A PENNY! OKAY?...."

"IT'S CALLED A UKE, JOEY. IT'S LIKE A GUITAR THAT DIDN'T GROW UP."

"HOW DO YOU LIKE OUR NEW CLUBHOUSE, MOM?"

"I'LL HELP YA, LADY! LET'S TRY THIS ONE ON FOR SIZE!"

"OPERATOR? LISTEN, I WANT YA TO SAY 'HELLO' TO A
LITTLE KID WHO'S NEVER BEEN ON THE TELEPHONE BEFORE!"

"GEE WHIZ! WHY DO YA WANNA MOVE, MR. WILSON? THIS IS A *SWELL* PLACE TO LIVE!"

"I'M NOT LOOKING FOR TROUBLE, HENRY. ALL I WANT TO DO IS MOVE, BUT NOW HE'S HIDDEN MY FOR SALE SIGN!"

"ARE YOU TRYIN' TO TELL ME MR. WILSON WANTS TO MOVE ON ACCOUNT OF *ME*? YOU'RE *CRAZY!*"

"HONEST, MR. WILSON! I WON'T *EVER* HIDE ROCKS IN YOUR UKULELE AGAIN!"

"MR. WILSON SAID I WAS A 'FINE LITTLE GENTLEMAN' AND *PATTED MY HEAD!* BUT THE PEOPLE DIDN'T BUY HIS HOUSE."

"IT'S CALLED A THER-MO-STRAT. IT'S A THING
MOM PUSHES *UP* AND DAD PUSHES *DOWN!*"

"GEE WHIZ! IF IT'S OKAY WITH RUFF, IT OUGHTA BE OKAY WITH *YOU* PEOPLE!"

"....AND HE NOT ONLY REFUSED TO SING, BUT HE TOLD ME IF I WANTED MUSIC, I COULD BUY A *RADIO!*"

"DID YOU 'MEMBER TO TELL YOUR WIFE THAT I LIKE SWEET PICKLES BETTER'N SOUR ONES?"

".... AND TELL MRS. TAYLOR SHE SHOULDN'T HATE DOGS, JUST 'CAUSE SHE'S GOT A CAT."

"WHO *SAYS* I GOTTA STAY IN BED?"

"JUST CHECKIN'."

"I SURE HOPE YOU DON'T STIR UP INJUN TROUBLE WITH ALL THOSE SMOKE SIGNALS!"

"WE SMOKED HEAP BIG PEACE PIPE. AND IT *WORKED!* HE'S BEEN PEACEFUL AS A SAINT EVER SINCE!"

"WHEN I LOCK MY DOOR IT MEANS I DON'T WANNA SEE *ANYBODY!*

"I JUST WANTED TO TELL YOU I'M SORRY I GOT SO MAD. AN' I GOD BLESSED YA AFTER ALL."

"*PIG KNUCKLES!* DID YA HEAR THAT? SHE'S BUYIN' *PIG KNUCKLES!*"

"I JUST CAME DOWN TO HELP MR. WEEKS LOOK FOR HIS SHIRT!"

"BUT *WHY* WOULD YOU BUY A BROKEN LAMP? AND *WHY* WOULD YOU PAY FULL PRICE FOR A BROKEN ....OH...."

"HE'S **NOT** A MUTT! AN' HE SOUNDS AS GOOD AS THAT LADY IN THERE!"

"DID YOU NOTICE HOW INTERESTED DENNIS WAS IN THE DOCTOR'S CON-
VERSATION? I ACTUALLY THINK HE WAS PICKING UP A FEW THINGS!"

"GEE WHIZ! YOU MEAN *NONE* OF YOU GUYS HAS EVER BEEN SHOT *ANYWHERE?*"

"HEY, DAD! YA WANNA BE *NEXT?*"

"MARGARET SAYS THE COW NEVER *LIVED* THAT COULD JUMP OVER THE MOON!"

"I DIDN'T 'SPECT YOU TO USE A FORK. MOM SAID YOU ATE LIKE A 'BIRD'!"

"THERE ARE FOUR PLATES BECAUSE DADDY IS BRINGING A FRIEND HOME FOR DINNER. RUFF IS *NOT* INVITED!"

"I'M TAKIN' ALONG A BOTTLE OF CATSUP! YOU NEVER GET MY SANDWICHES *RED* ENOUGH!"

"BOY, A REAL HORSE! BOY! HE'S A BEAUTY! OH, BOY!...YOU GO FIRST."

"WE CAME BY TO CHEER YA UP, UNCLE AL, 'CAUSE THE DOCTOR SAYS YOU'RE NOT DOIN' TOO GOOD!"

'GOT YA!'

"I DON'T KNOW HER NUMBER. BUT HER NAME IS MARGARET AN' SHE WEARS GLASSES!"

"BETTER ROLL UP YOUR PANTSCUFFS IF YOU'RE COMING IN *HERE!*"

"IT'S CALLED A COWLICK. I WAS BORN ON A CATTLE RANCH."

"HEY, I GOT AN IDEA! WHY DON'T WE HAVE A LITTLE SNACK BEFORE LUNCH?"

"I JUST WANTED TO SEE IF YOU WAS ALL
RIGHT. I DREAMED I BEAT YA UP!"

"THE TROUBLE IS, ALMOST *ALL* THAT WATER IS OVER MY HEAD!"

"I'M OILIN' THE BALLS!"

"BOY, YOU SURE GET *EXCITED* AT A BALL GAME!"

"I'LL NEVER FORGET THE DAY I GOT THIS MOON ROCKET SPACE LAUNCHER. DAD AND MR. WILSON BROKE IT!"

"HOW MUCH WOULD YA CHARGE TO BUILD A
HOUSE FOR A WHITE RAT NAMED FLOYD?"

"BOY, I'LL BET YOU'VE GOT THE *PRETTIEST* TOOL HANDLES IN THE *WHOLE NEIGHBORHOOD* NOW, MR. WILSON!"

"WE DON'T *WANT* ANY 'NICE CARROTS' FROM YOUR OWN GARDEN! WE *HATE* CARROTS! . . . . ."

"COUNTIN' MY MONEY. THE GUY ON TELEBISHION SAID WE COULD HAVE A SWIMMIN' POOL FOR 'JUST A FEW PENNIES A DAY'."

"ALL RIGHT! *ALL RIGHT!* RUFF NEEDS A TOOTHBRUSH. BUT DON'T HANG IT IN *HERE!*"

"THEY ALL HAVE PAPERS."

"YEAH. BUT WILL THEY *USE* 'EM?"

" 'It's *MY* PIGGY BANK AN' IT'S *MY* MONEY,'
THAT'S WHAT I SHOULDA SAID!"

"BOY, THAT WAS *REALLY* A LOUD ROAR, HUH, JOEY?
JOEY? *HEY, JOEY!*.....

"COME ON, DAD! I WANNA *PROVE* YOU CAN LIFT
TWO HUNDERD POUNDS!"

"I FEEL FOR YOU, PAL, BUT I CAN'T HIDE ALL MY TURNIPS JUST BECAUSE YOUR MOTHER MIGHT BUY SOME!"

"WHY DIDN'T YA *ASK* ME IF I WAS CHEWIN' BUBBLE GUM?"

"DON'T GET TOO CLOSE, JOEY. HIS HOSE WORKS *BOTH* WAYS!"

"Pssst! Make that a hotdog 'stead of ham, an' root beer 'stead of milk!"

"YOU BETTER WATCH OUT FOR ALLIGATORS!"

"I'LL HAVE IT OVER *HERE*, PLEASE!"

"DON'T WORRY, MOM. I WON'T BREAK ANYTHING UNTIL YOU'RE HOME TO SWEEP IT UP!"

"WOULDN'T IT BE KEEN IF IT *SNOWED*?"

"I'M GONNA GET A JOB CLEANIN' SWIMMIN' POOLS...
WHEN I LEARN HOW TO SWIM."

"YOU PEOPLE SURE DON'T LOOK LIKE MR. AN' MRS. WILSON!"

"MOM, WHERE DID YA HIDE THE WALNUTS?"

"WE DIDN'T GET ANY *MILK*, AN' WE DIDN'T GET ANY *NEWSPAPER!*"

"*LOOK, MOM!* DAD'S COOKIN' A *WHOLE BREAKFAST* WITHOUT PLUGGIN' IN A *SINGLE* THING!"

"HELLO, GRANDPA? LISTEN, WHY DON'T YA COME OVER AN' SPOIL ME FOR A FEW DAYS?"

"LOOK WHAT GRANDPA BROUGHT ME! *BONGO DRUMS!*"

"ALL I SAID WAS 'HERE KITTY, KITTY, KITTY!' AN' *BOY!*"

"WE'RE BACK FROM OUR CAMPIN' TRIP! I GUESS YOU WANNA HEAR *ALL ABOUT IT!?*"

'WOW! I MUST BE GROWIN'! I NEVER SEEN *THAT* NUMBER BEFORE!'

"HOW DO *YOU* KNOW ALL I GOT IN MY PIGGY BANK IS SLUGS?"

"MOM! TAKE A LOOK AT *THIS* GUY! AN' HE SAYS HE *NEVER* DRINKS MILK!"

"YOU BOYS CERTAINLY GET YOUR *MONEY'S WORTH* OUT OF A WADING POOL!"

"I'M NOT GONNA CALL YOU 'MISS WADE'! AN' *STOP*
CALLIN' ME '*SONNY*'!"

"MY DADDY'S REAL STRONG! YOU OUGHTA
SEE HIM BEND BEER CANS!"

"WANNA HAVE A LITTLE FUN? I GOTTA *EXTRA* YO-YO!"

"BOY, YOU SURE MUST HAVE A *LONG* CLOTHESLINE!"

"I WONDER WHAT THEY DO WHEN THE BASEMENT GETS FULL OF STEPS?"

"BUT IT'S ALL RIGHT FOR _YOU_ TO HAVE A **BIG** ONE HANGING OVER THE FIREPLACE!"

"AN' WHEN OL' MARGARET SAYS 'LET'S PLAY POST OFFICE', I'M GONNA STICK THIS STAMP ON THE END OF HER NOSE!"

"WHO WANTS TO GIVE MY MOM A SEAT
'FORE I STAND ON HIS SHOE?"